Christmas Gift Tracker

belongs to

....

About this notebook

This Christmas notebook was created to help you find the right gift for your loved ones.

It is divided into sections that will make buying a gift a pleasure.

In the notebook, you will find parts such as:

- Name
- About
- Interests
- Preferences
- Gift Ideas from Stores
- Gift Ideas from Websites
- Purchased Gift

Useful information:

Description of the person:

Pay special attention to the "About" section, in which try to write a few words about your loved ones (describe them).
Then think about her / his interests and what she/he likes to do (preferences).
When you fill in the parts above it will be easier for you to find the right gift.   :)

Gift search:

The "Gift Ideas from Stores" section will allow you to note down essential information about potential gifts that catch your eye during your shopping in town.

The "Gift Ideas from Websites" section will certainly come in handy when searching the internet.

Decision-making:

Under the "Purchased Gifts" section, you will be able to note what you purchased during the season and how much money you spent on it.

Most importantly, this gift tracker will also come in handy next year;) and maybe the year after that. It will help you remember what you bought last season and not repeat the same gift. You will also find notes about other gifts that you found earlier but didn't buy. You will already know where to buy them and save valuable time.

Get started!!!

Christmas Gift Tracker

Name : ....

About

Interests:

-
-
-
-
-

Preferences:

-
-
-
-

Gift Ideas from Stores:

Type of gift:	Place to buy:	Price:

Gift Ideas from Websites:

Type of gift:	Website:	Price:

Purchased Gifts:

Type of gift	Purchased in year/season	Amount spent

Christmas Gift Tracker

Name : ....

Interests:

-
-
-
-

Preferences:

-
-
-
-

Gift Ideas from Stores:

Type of gift:	Place to buy:	Price:

Gift Ideas from Websites:

Type of gift:	Website:	Price:

Purchased Gifts:

Type of gift	Purchased in year/season	Amount spent

Christmas Gift Tracker

Name : ....

About

Interests:

-
-
-
-
-

Preferences:

-
-
-
-
-

Gift Ideas from Stores:

Type of gift:	Place to buy:	Price:

Gift Ideas from Websites:

Type of gift:	Website:	Price:

Purchased Gifts:

Type of gift	Purchased in year/season	Amount spent

Christmas Gift Tracker

Name : ....

About

Interests:

-
-
-
-
-
-
-
-

Preferences:

-
-
-
-
-
-

Gift Ideas from Stores:

Type of gift:	Place to buy:	Price:

Gift Ideas from Websites:

Type of gift:	Website:	Price:

Purchased Gifts:

Type of gift	Purchased in year/season	Amount spent

Christmas Gift Tracker

Name : ....

About

Interests:

-
-
-
-
-
-

Preferences:

-
-
-
-
-
-

Gift Ideas from Stores:

Type of gift:	Place to buy:	Price:

Gift Ideas from Websites:

Type of gift:	Website:	Price:

Purchased Gifts:

Type of gift	Purchased in year/season	Amount spent

Christmas Gift Tracker

Name : ....

About

Interests:

-
-
-
-
-

Preferences:

-
-
-
-

Gift Ideas from Stores:

Type of gift:	Place to buy:	Price:

Gift Ideas from Websites:

Type of gift:	Website:	Price:

Purchased Gifts:

Type of gift	Purchased in year/season	Amount spent

Christmas Gift Tracker

Name : ....

About

Interests:

-
-
-
-

Preferences:

-
-
-
-

Gift Ideas from Stores:

Type of gift:	Place to buy:	Price:

Gift Ideas from Websites:

Type of gift:	Website:	Price:

Purchased Gifts:

Type of gift	Purchased in year/season	Amount spent

Christmas Gift Tracker

Name : ....

About

Interests:

-
-
-
-
-
-
-

Preferences:

-
-
-
-
-
-
-

Gift Ideas from Stores:

Type of gift:	Place to buy:	Price:

Gift Ideas from Websites:

Type of gift:	Website:	Price:

Purchased Gifts:

Type of gift	Purchased in year/season	Amount spent

Christmas Gift Tracker

Name : ....

About

Interests:

-
-
-
-
-

Preferences:

-
-
-
-
-

Gift Ideas from Stores:

Type of gift:	Place to buy:	Price:

Gift Ideas from Websites:

Type of gift:	Website:	Price:

Purchased Gifts:

Type of gift	Purchased in year/season	Amount spent

Christmas Gift Tracker

Name : ....

About

Interests:

-
-
-
-
-
-
-

Preferences:

-
-
-
-
-
-

Gift Ideas from Stores:

Type of gift:	Place to buy:	Price:

Gift Ideas from Websites:

Type of gift:	Website:	Price:

Purchased Gifts:

Type of gift	Purchased in year/season	Amount spent

Christmas Gift Tracker

Name : ....

Interests:

-
-
-
-

Preferences:

-
-
-
-

Gift Ideas from Stores:

Type of gift:	Place to buy:	Price:

Gift Ideas from Websites:

Type of gift:	Website:	Price:

Purchased Gifts:

Type of gift	Purchased in year/season	Amount spent

Christmas Gift Tracker

Name : ....

About

Interests:

-
-
-
-
-
-

Preferences:

-
-
-
-
-
-

Gift Ideas from Stores:

Type of gift:	Place to buy:	Price:

Gift Ideas from Websites:

Type of gift:	Website:	Price:

Purchased Gifts:

Type of gift	Purchased in year/season	Amount spent

Christmas Gift Tracker

Name : ....

About

Interests:

-
-
-
-
-
-

Preferences:

-
-
-
-
-

Gift Ideas from Stores:

Type of gift:	Place to buy:	Price:

Gift Ideas from Websites:

Type of gift:	Website:	Price:

Purchased Gifts:

Type of gift	Purchased in year/season	Amount spent

Christmas Gift Tracker

Name : ....

Interests:

-
-
-
-
-
-

Preferences:

-
-
-
-

Gift Ideas from Stores:

Type of gift:	Place to buy:	Price:

Gift Ideas from Websites:

Type of gift:	Website:	Price:

Purchased Gifts:

Type of gift	Purchased in year/season	Amount spent

Christmas Gift Tracker

Name : ....

Interests:

-
-
-
-
-
-
-

Preferences:

-
-
-
-
-
-

Gift Ideas from Stores:

Type of gift:	Place to buy:	Price:

Gift Ideas from Websites:

Type of gift:	Website:	Price:

Purchased Gifts:

Type of gift	Purchased in year/season	Amount spent

Christmas Gift Tracker

Name : ....

About

Interests:

-
-
-
-
-
-
-

Preferences:

-
-
-
-
-
-
-

Gift Ideas from Stores:

Type of gift:	Place to buy:	Price:

Gift Ideas from Websites:

Type of gift:	Website:	Price:

Purchased Gifts:

Type of gift	Purchased in year/season	Amount spent

Christmas Gift Tracker

Name : ....

About

Interests:

-
-
-
-
-
-
-

Preferences:

-
-
-
-
-

Gift Ideas from Stores:

Type of gift:	Place to buy:	Price:

Gift Ideas from Websites:

Type of gift:	Website:	Price:

Purchased Gifts:

Type of gift	Purchased in year/season	Amount spent

Christmas Gift Tracker

Name : ....

Interests:

-
-
-
-
-
-
-

Preferences:

-
-
-
-
-
-
-

Gift Ideas from Stores:

Type of gift:	Place to buy:	Price:

Gift Ideas from Websites:

Type of gift:	Website:	Price:

Purchased Gifts:

Type of gift	Purchased in year/season	Amount spent

Christmas Gift Tracker

Name : ....

About

Interests:

-
-
-
-
-
-
-

Preferences:

-
-
-
-
-
-

Gift Ideas from Stores:

Type of gift:	Place to buy:	Price:

Gift Ideas from Websites:

Type of gift:	Website:	Price:

Purchased Gifts:

Type of gift	Purchased in year/season	Amount spent

Christmas Gift Tracker

Name : ....

About

Interests:

-
-
-
-
-
-
-

Preferences:

-
-
-
-
-

Gift Ideas from Stores:

Type of gift:	Place to buy:	Price:

Gift Ideas from Websites:

Type of gift:	Website:	Price:

Purchased Gifts:

Type of gift	Purchased in year/season	Amount spent

Christmas Gift Tracker

Name : ....

About

Interests:
-
-
-
-
-
-

Preferences:
-
-
-
-
-

Gift Ideas from Stores:

Type of gift:	Place to buy:	Price:

Gift Ideas from Websites:

Type of gift:	Website:	Price:

Purchased Gifts:

Type of gift	Purchased in year/season	Amount spent

Christmas Gift Tracker

Name : ....

About

Interests:

-
-
-
-
-
-
-

Preferences:

-
-
-
-
-
-
-

Gift Ideas from Stores:

Type of gift:	Place to buy:	Price:

Gift Ideas from Websites:

Type of gift:	Website:	Price:

Purchased Gifts:

Type of gift	Purchased in year/season	Amount spent

Christmas Gift Tracker

Name : ....

About

Interests:

-
-
-
-
-
-
-

Preferences:

-
-
-
-
-
-

Gift Ideas from Stores:

Type of gift:	Place to buy:	Price:

Gift Ideas from Websites:

Type of gift:	Website:	Price:

Purchased Gifts:

Type of gift	Purchased in year/season	Amount spent

Christmas Gift Tracker

Name : ....

About

Interests:

-
-
-
-
-
-

Preferences:

-
-
-
-
-

Gift Ideas from Stores:

Type of gift:	Place to buy:	Price:

Gift Ideas from Websites:

Type of gift:	Website:	Price:

Purchased Gifts:

Type of gift	Purchased in year/season	Amount spent

Christmas Gift Tracker

Name : ....

About

Interests:

-
-
-
-
-
-

Preferences:

-
-
-
-
-
-

Gift Ideas from Stores:

Type of gift:	Place to buy:	Price:

Gift Ideas from Websites:

Type of gift:	Website:	Price:

Purchased Gifts:

Type of gift	Purchased in year/season	Amount spent

Christmas Gift Tracker

Name : ....

About

Interests:

-
-
-
-
-
-

Preferences:

-
-
-
-
-

Gift Ideas from Stores:

Type of gift:	Place to buy:	Price:

Gift Ideas from Websites:

Type of gift:	Website:	Price:

Purchased Gifts:

Type of gift	Purchased in year/season	Amount spent

Christmas Gift Tracker

Name : ....

About

Interests:

-
-
-
-
-

Preferences:

-
-
-
-

Gift Ideas from Stores:

Type of gift:	Place to buy:	Price:

Gift Ideas from Websites:

Type of gift:	Website:	Price:

Purchased Gifts:

Type of gift	Purchased in year/season	Amount spent

Christmas Gift Tracker

Name : ....

Interests:

-
-
-
-
-
-
-

Preferences:

-
-
-
-
-
-

Gift Ideas from Stores:

Type of gift:	Place to buy:	Price:

Gift Ideas from Websites:

Type of gift:	Website:	Price:

Purchased Gifts:

Type of gift	Purchased in year/season	Amount spent

Christmas Gift Tracker

Name : ....

About

Interests:

-
-
-
-
-
-

Preferences:

-
-
-
-
-

Gift Ideas from Stores:

Type of gift:	Place to buy:	Price:

Gift Ideas from Websites:

Type of gift:	Website:	Price:

Purchased Gifts:

Type of gift	Purchased in year/season	Amount spent

Christmas Gift Tracker

Name : ....

About

Interests:

-
-
-
-
-
-
-

Preferences:

-
-
-
-
-
-

Gift Ideas from Stores:

Type of gift:	Place to buy:	Price:

Gift Ideas from Websites:

Type of gift:	Website:	Price:

Purchased Gifts:

Type of gift	Purchased in year/season	Amount spent

Christmas Gift Tracker

Name : ....

Interests:

-
-
-
-
-
-
-

Preferences:

-
-
-
-
-

Gift Ideas from Stores:

Type of gift:	Place to buy:	Price:

Gift Ideas from Websites:

Type of gift:	Website:	Price:

Purchased Gifts:

Type of gift	Purchased in year/season	Amount spent

Christmas Gift Tracker

Name : ....

About

Interests:

-
-
-
-
-
-
-

Preferences:

-
-
-
-
-

Gift Ideas from Stores:

Type of gift:	Place to buy:	Price:

Gift Ideas from Websites:

Type of gift:	Website:	Price:

Purchased Gifts:

Type of gift	Purchased in year/season	Amount spent

Christmas Gift Tracker

Name : ....

About

Interests:

-
-
-
-
-
-
-

Preferences:

-
-
-
-
-
-

Gift Ideas from Stores:

Type of gift:	Place to buy:	Price:

Gift Ideas from Websites:

Type of gift:	Website:	Price:

Purchased Gifts:

Type of gift	Purchased in year/season	Amount spent

Christmas Gift Tracker

Name : ....

About

Interests:

-
-
-
-
-
-

Preferences:

-
-
-
-
-
-

Gift Ideas from Stores:

Type of gift:	Place to buy:	Price:

Gift Ideas from Websites:

Type of gift:	Website:	Price:

Purchased Gifts:

Type of gift	Purchased in year/season	Amount spent

Christmas Gift Tracker

Name : ....

About

Interests:

-
-
-
-

Preferences:

-
-
-
-

Gift Ideas from Stores:

Type of gift:	Place to buy:	Price:

Gift Ideas from Websites:

Type of gift:	Website:	Price:

Purchased Gifts:

Type of gift	Purchased in year/season	Amount spent

Christmas Gift Tracker

Name : ....

Interests:

-
-
-
-

Preferences:

-
-
-
-

Gift Ideas from Stores:

Type of gift:	Place to buy:	Price:

Gift Ideas from Websites:

Type of gift:	Website:	Price:

Purchased Gifts:

Type of gift	Purchased in year/season	Amount spent

Christmas Gift Tracker

Name : ....

Interests:

-
-
-
-
-
-
-

Preferences:

-
-
-
-
-
-

Gift Ideas from Stores:

Type of gift:	Place to buy:	Price:

Gift Ideas from Websites:

Type of gift:	Website:	Price:

Purchased Gifts:

Type of gift	Purchased in year/season	Amount spent

Christmas Gift Tracker

Name : ....

About

Interests:

-
-
-
-
-
-
-

Preferences:

-
-
-
-
-
-

Gift Ideas from Stores:

Type of gift:	Place to buy:	Price:

Gift Ideas from Websites:

Type of gift:	Website:	Price:

Purchased Gifts:

Type of gift	Purchased in year/season	Amount spent

Christmas Gift Tracker

Name : ....

About

Interests:

-
-
-
-
-

Preferences:

-
-
-
-
-

Gift Ideas from Stores:

Type of gift:	Place to buy:	Price:

Gift Ideas from Websites:

Type of gift:	Website:	Price:

Purchased Gifts:

Type of gift	Purchased in year/season	Amount spent

Christmas Gift Tracker

Name : ....

Interests:

-
-
-
-
-
-
-

Preferences:

-
-
-
-
-
-

Gift Ideas from Stores:

Type of gift:	Place to buy:	Price:

Gift Ideas from Websites:

Type of gift:	Website:	Price:

Purchased Gifts:

Type of gift	Purchased in year/season	Amount spent

Christmas Gift Tracker

Name : ....

Interests:

-
-
-
-
-
-

Preferences:

-
-
-
-
-

Gift Ideas from Stores:

Type of gift:	Place to buy:	Price:

Gift Ideas from Websites:

Type of gift:	Website:	Price:

Purchased Gifts:

Type of gift	Purchased in year/season	Amount spent

Christmas Gift Tracker

Name : ....

About

Interests:

-
-
-
-
-

Preferences:

-
-
-
-
-

Gift Ideas from Stores:

Type of gift:	Place to buy:	Price:

Gift Ideas from Websites:

Type of gift:	Website:	Price:

Purchased Gifts:

Type of gift	Purchased in year/season	Amount spent

Christmas Gift Tracker

Name : ....

About

Interests:

-
-
-
-
-
-
-

Preferences:

-
-
-
-
-
-
-

Gift Ideas from Stores:

Type of gift:	Place to buy:	Price:

Gift Ideas from Websites:

Type of gift:	Website:	Price:

Purchased Gifts:

Type of gift	Purchased in year/season	Amount spent

Christmas Gift Tracker

Name : ....

Interests:

-
-
-
-
-

Preferences:

-
-
-
-
-

Gift Ideas from Stores:

Type of gift:	Place to buy:	Price:

Gift Ideas from Websites:

Type of gift:	Website:	Price:

Purchased Gifts:

Type of gift	Purchased in year/season	Amount spent

Christmas Gift Tracker

Name : ....

About

Interests:

-
-
-
-
-
-
-

Preferences:

-
-
-
-
-
-

Gift Ideas from Stores:

Type of gift:	Place to buy:	Price:

Gift Ideas from Websites:

Type of gift:	Website:	Price:

Purchased Gifts:

Type of gift	Purchased in year/season	Amount spent

Christmas Gift Tracker

Name : ....

About

Interests:

-
-
-
-
-
-
-

Preferences:

-
-
-
-
-
-

Gift Ideas from Stores:

Type of gift:	Place to buy:	Price:

Gift Ideas from Websites:

Type of gift:	Website:	Price:

Purchased Gifts:

Type of gift	Purchased in year/season	Amount spent

Christmas Gift Tracker

Name : ....

Interests:

-
-
-
-
-
-

Preferences:

-
-
-
-
-
-

Gift Ideas from Stores:

Type of gift:	Place to buy:	Price:

Gift Ideas from Websites:

Type of gift:	Website:	Price:

Purchased Gifts:

Type of gift	Purchased in year/season	Amount spent

Christmas Gift Tracker

Name : ....

Interests:

-
-
-
-
-
-

Preferences:

-
-
-
-
-

Gift Ideas from Stores:

Type of gift:	Place to buy:	Price:

Gift Ideas from Websites:

Type of gift:	Website:	Price:

Purchased Gifts:

Type of gift	Purchased in year/season	Amount spent

Christmas Gift Tracker

Name : ....

Interests:

-
-
-
-
-
-

Preferences:

-
-
-
-

Gift Ideas from Stores:

Type of gift:	Place to buy:	Price:

Gift Ideas from Websites:

Type of gift:	Website:	Price:

Purchased Gifts:

Type of gift	Purchased in year/season	Amount spent

Christmas Gift Tracker

Name : ....

Interests:

-
-
-
-
-
-

Preferences:

-
-
-
-

Gift Ideas from Stores:

Type of gift:	Place to buy:	Price:

Gift Ideas from Websites:

Type of gift:	Website:	Price:

Purchased Gifts:

Type of gift	Purchased in year/season	Amount spent

Christmas Gift Tracker

Name : ....

About

Interests:

-
-
-
-
-

Preferences:

-
-
-
-
-

Gift Ideas from Stores:

Type of gift:	Place to buy:	Price:

Gift Ideas from Websites:

Type of gift:	Website:	Price:

Purchased Gifts:

Type of gift	Purchased in year/season	Amount spent

Christmas Gift Tracker

Name : ....

About

Interests:

-
-
-
-
-
-
-

Preferences:

-
-
-
-
-
-

Gift Ideas from Stores:

Type of gift:	Place to buy:	Price:

Gift Ideas from Websites:

Type of gift:	Website:	Price:

Purchased Gifts:

Type of gift	Purchased in year/season	Amount spent

Christmas Gift Tracker

Name : ....

Interests:

-
-
-
-
-
-
-

Preferences:

-
-
-
-
-
-

Gift Ideas from Stores:

Type of gift:	Place to buy:	Price:

Gift Ideas from Websites:

Type of gift:	Website:	Price:

Purchased Gifts:

Type of gift	Purchased in year/season	Amount spent

Christmas Gift Tracker

Name : ....

About

Interests:

-
-
-
-
-

Preferences:

-
-
-
-
-

Gift Ideas from Stores:

Type of gift:	Place to buy:	Price:

Gift Ideas from Websites:

Type of gift:	Website:	Price:

Purchased Gifts:

Type of gift	Purchased in year/season	Amount spent

Christmas Gift Tracker

Name : ....

About

Interests:

-
-
-
-
-
-

Preferences:

-
-
-
-
-
-

Gift Ideas from Stores:

Type of gift:	Place to buy:	Price:

Gift Ideas from Websites:

Type of gift:	Website:	Price:

Purchased Gifts:

Type of gift	Purchased in year/season	Amount spent

Christmas Gift Tracker

Name : ....

About

Interests:

-
-
-
-
-

Preferences:

-
-
-
-
-

Gift Ideas from Stores:

Type of gift:	Place to buy:	Price:

Gift Ideas from Websites:

Type of gift:	Website:	Price:

Purchased Gifts:

Type of gift	Purchased in year/season	Amount spent

Christmas Gift Tracker

Name : ....

Interests:

-
-
-
-
-

Preferences:

-
-
-
-
-

Gift Ideas from Stores:

Type of gift:	Place to buy:	Price:

Gift Ideas from Websites:

Type of gift:	Website:	Price:

Purchased Gifts:

Type of gift	Purchased in year/season	Amount spent

Christmas Gift Tracker

Name : ....

About

Interests:

-
-
-
-
-
-
-

Preferences:

-
-
-
-
-

Gift Ideas from Stores:

Type of gift:	Place to buy:	Price:

Gift Ideas from Websites:

Type of gift:	Website:	Price:

Purchased Gifts:

Type of gift	Purchased in year/season	Amount spent

Christmas Gift Tracker

Name : ....

Interests:

-
-
-
-

Preferences:

-
-
-
-

Gift Ideas from Stores:

Type of gift:	Place to buy:	Price:

Gift Ideas from Websites:

Type of gift:	Website:	Price:

Purchased Gifts:

Type of gift	Purchased in year/season	Amount spent

Christmas Gift Tracker

Name : ....

About

Interests:

-
-
-
-
-
-

Preferences:

-
-
-
-

Gift Ideas from Stores:

Type of gift:	Place to buy:	Price:

Gift Ideas from Websites:

Type of gift:	Website:	Price:

Purchased Gifts:

Type of gift	Purchased in year/season	Amount spent

Christmas Gift Tracker

Name : ....

About

Interests:

-
-
-
-

Preferences:

-
-
-
-

Gift Ideas from Stores:

Type of gift:	Place to buy:	Price:

Gift Ideas from Websites:

Type of gift:	Website:	Price:

Purchased Gifts:

Type of gift	Purchased in year/season	Amount spent

Christmas Gift Tracker

Name : ....

Interests:

-
-
-
-
-
-
-

Preferences:

-
-
-
-
-
-
-

Gift Ideas from Stores:

Type of gift:	Place to buy:	Price:

Gift Ideas from Websites:

Type of gift:	Website:	Price:

Purchased Gifts:

Type of gift	Purchased in year/season	Amount spent

Christmas Gift Tracker

Name : ....

Interests:

-
-
-
-
-
-

Preferences:

-
-
-
-
-
-

Gift Ideas from Stores:

Type of gift:	Place to buy:	Price:

Gift Ideas from Websites:

Type of gift:	Website:	Price:

Purchased Gifts:

Type of gift	Purchased in year/season	Amount spent

Christmas Gift Tracker

Name : ....

Interests:

-
-
-
-
-
-
-

Preferences:

-
-
-
-
-

Gift Ideas from Stores:

Type of gift:	Place to buy:	Price:

Gift Ideas from Websites:

Type of gift:	Website:	Price:

Purchased Gifts:

Type of gift	Purchased in year/season	Amount spent

Christmas Gift Tracker

Name : ....

About

Interests:

-
-
-
-
-
-

Preferences:

-
-
-
-
-

Gift Ideas from Stores:

Type of gift:	Place to buy:	Price:

Gift Ideas from Websites:

Type of gift:	Website:	Price:

Purchased Gifts:

Type of gift	Purchased in year/season	Amount spent

Christmas Gift Tracker

Name : ....

Interests:

-
-
-
-
-
-

Preferences:

-
-
-
-
-
-

Gift Ideas from Stores:

Type of gift:	Place to buy:	Price:

Gift Ideas from Websites:

Type of gift:	Website:	Price:

Purchased Gifts:

Type of gift	Purchased in year/season	Amount spent

Christmas Gift Tracker

Name : ....

About

Interests:

-
-
-
-
-
-
-

Preferences:

-
-
-
-
-
-

Gift Ideas from Stores:

Type of gift:	Place to buy:	Price:

Gift Ideas from Websites:

Type of gift:	Website:	Price:

Purchased Gifts:

Type of gift	Purchased in year/season	Amount spent

Christmas Gift Tracker

Name : ....

Interests:

-
-
-
-
-
-
-

Preferences:

-
-
-
-
-

Gift Ideas from Stores:

Type of gift:	Place to buy:	Price:

Gift Ideas from Websites:

Type of gift:	Website:	Price:

Purchased Gifts:

Type of gift	Purchased in year/season	Amount spent

Christmas Gift Tracker

Name : ....

Interests:

-
-
-
-
-
-

Preferences:

-
-
-
-
-
-

Gift Ideas from Stores:

Type of gift:	Place to buy:	Price:

Gift Ideas from Websites:

Type of gift:	Website:	Price:

Purchased Gifts:

Type of gift	Purchased in year/season	Amount spent

Christmas Gift Tracker

Name : ....

Interests:

-
-
-
-
-

Preferences:

-
-
-
-
-

Gift Ideas from Stores:

Type of gift:	Place to buy:	Price:

Gift Ideas from Websites:

Type of gift:	Website:	Price:

Purchased Gifts:

Type of gift	Purchased in year/season	Amount spent

Christmas Gift Tracker

Name : ....

Interests:

-
-
-
-

Preferences:

-
-
-
-

Gift Ideas from Stores:

Type of gift:	Place to buy:	Price:

Gift Ideas from Websites:

Type of gift:	Website:	Price:

Purchased Gifts:

Type of gift	Purchased in year/season	Amount spent

Christmas Gift Tracker

Name : ....

Interests:

-
-
-
-
-
-

Preferences:

-
-
-
-
-

Gift Ideas from Stores:

Type of gift:	Place to buy:	Price:

Gift Ideas from Websites:

Type of gift:	Website:	Price:

Purchased Gifts:

Type of gift	Purchased in year/season	Amount spent

Made in the USA
Monee, IL
15 November 2024

70233535R00085